POSTINGS

POSTINGS

Jim McCue

PALLAS ATHENE

Hastings Pier formerly owned by an offshore company

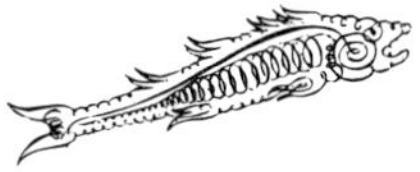

'You are giving a wrong impression of yourself. At least I trust you are.'

'Well I hope I seem to be.'

Ivy Compton-Burnett,
A Heritage and its History

Only Donne cited by OED for
inter-assured
interbring
intercharge
intertouch
interwish
and
inter-accuse

'I met ten students,
seven of them diverse.'
David Lammy

De Quincey
Skeletons 'absolutely *de trop*
in good society'

Dog-walker in the woods
explaining what his
bracelet does:
'It tells you how many steps
you've taken, and that you
need to exercise if you are
too sedimentary.'

'Your browser is deprecated.
Please upgrade.'

Nansi
Georgea
Aliz
Filipa
Leesa
Sybelle
Kait
Barbora
Amba
Emeli
Emilie
Salli

'She goes to confession every Saturday—except the week I was there—she couldn't think of any sins.'

Lily Yeats to J. B. Yeats

Website for Betty's teashop & patisserie:

'Allow all cookies.'

Titles (mostly remaindered):
Darwin's Finches
Darwin's Ghosts
Darwin's Unfinished Symphony
Darwin's Backyard
Darwin's Devices
Darwin's Island

'We've gone into this downward spiral of escalation.'
Radio 4

It's as in sleep,
in the quiet of the night,
Our languid eyelids close
and in their dream
Won't tell wherever we are
nor where we're going
Or trying not to go nor can
we get there where-
Ever where might be, and
who knows who it is
We maybe are . . .

David Ferry, Æneid XII

‘Chew one tablet
twice daily.’

Part I exam at Cambridge,
formerly known as
‘The Previous Examination’

'My wife's forty and
she's certainly still worth
a second glans.'

Despite the need for runs
'Buttler flailed to score.'

Murderpedia

The Children of Mary held their meetings in the convent, and appeared in public in blue cloaks and long white veils, singing. I suppose it was some sort of virginity action group.

George O'Brien,
The Village of Longing

South Koreans going north to meet relatives with a sense of 'intrepidation'

BBC World Service

Employee told in 'industrial language' that he's a 'bald c***'. Court upholds his claim to be offended by sexism, because baldness is predominantly male.

Never take an iambus as a Christian name.

Samuel Taylor Coleridge

Increase in rate of inflation significantly due to rises in the price of computer games

'Next to her was a lady in blue, with a face.'

Clarice Lispector

Brecon Beacon
demoted to a hill

'A model employee, fulfilling his allotted task with an exemplary absence of initiative'
Émile Zola

Woman who once had
'a brush with James Dyson'

Times Literary Supplement (New Style):

Go and (re-)read *The Garden of Forking Paths*: it's fantastic . . . *Red Thread* is in many ways rather a good book . . . I liked the line very much indeed . . . I was sorry that . . . You'll enjoy Higgins's sarcastic take-down . . . I can just about see why . . . I'm more sceptical about . . . Sure, Catullus 64 is ingeniously structured . . . Come off it.

Self-advertising man who
'hurries into fame
with all his might'
George Crabbe

Doctoral candidate in the Dept of Gender and Cultural Studies at the University of Sydney researching ocean environmental and juridical imaginaries

‘We can transform your existing staircase into something you can’t wait to come home to.’

‘It’s easy to keep a moustache indoors, in warm dry conditions.’

Cornelius Medvei,
The Making of Mr. Bolsover

UCL writing tutorial:

Compare the following two short texts, (A) and (B). How many differences do you see in the second text? What is the function/effect/purpose of each difference? You will probably notice that (B) is more 'academic', but it is important to understand why.

(A)

Extensive reading helps students to improve their vocabulary.

(B)

Research conducted by Yen (2005) appears to indicate that, for a significant proportion of students, extensive reading may contribute to an improvement in their active vocabulary. Yen's (2005) study involved learners aged 15-16 in the UK, although it may be applicable to other groups. However, the study involved an opt-in sample, which means that the sample students may have been more 'keen', or more involved in reading already. It would be useful to see whether the findings differ in a wider sample.

'dilapitated'

Exercise:
'preparation for circumstances that never come along'
Robert Musil,
The Man without Qualities

Theresa May wearing a length of chain as a neck-lace when visiting Nelson Mandela's prison cell

'How finely we argue
upon mistaken facts!'
Laurence Sterne, Tristram Shandy

'Route canal work'

'I completely resonate with
everything you share.'

'Only the profoundly vain, my friends, understand: no two mirrors are alike. And only we, the truly unapologetic, can name our especial favorites.'

Allan Gurganus,
Oldest Living Confederate Widow Tells All

‘He specializes in
anti-Semitism training.’
Radio 4

Four years into a doctorate on
‘The History of the Essay’
but not acquainted with
The Oxford Book of Essays

'He was not a nihilist for nothing.'
Ivan Sergeyevich Turgenev

Wikipedia:
'"Seven Types of Ambiguity" is an Australian television drama series on the ABC first screened on 13 April 2017. . .'

‘as false as stairs of sand’

Merchant of Venice

CV:

‘I also write about design, films and pop culture. I’ve made words do sentences for: . . .’

'Prostitutes perform a service to society by rendering men more "aimables, galans, entreprenans", by making the German less brutal, the Englishman less phlegmatic, the Spaniard less grave, the provincial less awkward, and young sons less timid.'

Réclamation addressée à
S. Ece. Mgr. Delavau,
préfet de police,
par Modeste Agnès,
patentée exerçant au Palais-Royal.
À Paris,
chez les marchands de nouveautés,
1821
(Quaritch catalogue)

‘The guest fully agreed
and said that,
to be sure,
there was no one like God.’

Fyodor Mikhailovich
Dostoyevsky

Interviewee:
'The long answer is
"Yes".'

Tax on single-use plastics might include chewing gum.

Netspell:

‘the powers at be’

‘next store’

‘local laundry mat’

‘sticks in his claw’

‘story being bounded about’

‘holly reefs’

‘irrelevant of my personal opinion’

‘all man or of outrange’

‘one in the same person’

‘nosey in running the country’

Bots not permitted:
Bodleian subscribers asked to
'confirm humanity'

Doubly reassuring to
be told that *both* sides
have reached a deal

'. . . some album named
"Music to Listen to Music By"'

Randall Jarrell

'. . . like being in a Renaissance
Italian court of the Borges. . .'

(clearly pronouncing Bor-kes)

Ian McEwen

Women's Land Speed Record..?

Cosmetics bottle:
'Protect & Moisture'
Ministry of state:
'Department for Digital, Culture,
Media and Sport'

[Adventures of] Peregrine Penis

(Anon., 1794)

Dentists

'charging through the nose'

'. . . went to Harvard Law,
never farted in his life,
he's our man.'

Brad Leithauser, Seaward

To list in order of boringness:

astronomy
Tolkien
motor-racing
The Titanic
dinosaurs
Melvyn Bragg discussing
The Mabinogion

Soup
'contained an egg,
which I thought irrelevant'
A. E. Housman

'He itinerated . . . '
Radio 4

Conference proposal:

'Do these women's graphic narratives, like those considered by Chute, also speak to dominant tropes associated with trauma and the theory thereof?'

All this being

'broadly understood'.

Very English:

'If it doesn't rain,
we're doing well.'

'I spent rather too much
[ie. hundreds],
but still, it is quite a nice book.'

'How did she do?'
'She was better in the first game
than the second.'

Midget Gem sweets
renamed
after campaign

West to draw
'a red line in the sand'

Even after *The Queen's Gambit*, not many women are playing chess. 'It's just not good enough.'

Henry VI, Part 2:
'A wilderness is populous enough'
Omar Khayyam XI:
'And Wilderness is Paradise enow'

Trump
'had a foreign policy that
focused on the rest of the
world.'
Spokeswoman

'On me':
'my choice'
'my responsibility'
'my fault'
'not my choice, or responsibility,
but unfairly foisted upon me'

What should the first movement
of Haydn's Symphony no. 83 be
'paired with'?
Radio 3

'. . . a lot of surprises, some
of them expected . . .'
Radio 4

Edward Mendelson:
'He adds critical distancing comments whenever he detects "a hint of misogyny or homophobia," as if to reassure censorious readers that he shares their sense of the moral urgency of scolding dead people.'

Opposite of absenteeism:
'presenteeism'

'. . . conditions which even Germans must have found insupportable without an audience'
Eric Newby, The Great Grain Race

‘When buying a car, people are looking for a legendary experience.’

INGANNATION:
cheat, fraud, deception, juggle, delusion, imposture, trick, sleight. A word neither used nor necessary.
Johnson’s Dictionary
(citing only Sir Thomas Browne)

‘Doubling down on gas’:
using more, or less?
‘Last best hope’:
best, or last?

Chesterton:

'A Liberal may be defined approximately as a man who, if he could by waving his hand in a dark room, stop the mouths of all the deceivers of mankind for ever, would not wave his hand. Browning was a Liberal in this sense.'

Irish Stock Exchange now Euronext Dublin

Actress on not voting for a female candidate:

'I don't vote with my vagina, you know; this is bigger than that.'

The Fortunes of Nigel
an impossible title

Radio 4:
report that alcohol shortens life:
'sobering' reading
anticipating military action in Syria:
'not rocket science'

Gutenberg Bible at Lambeth Palace believed to be the first printed book to arrive in Britain, on the basis of its illuminations, painted in a workshop in East Sheen

Los Angeles Review of Books
determined to 'diversify the
pipeline into publishing'

Prince, pardon me, or strike me
if you please,
I cannot be much lower
than my knees.
Pericles (Shakespeare and Anon.)

Two n's, two o's, two m's, two t's
and two l's:
noncommittally

'I can't see any way back for them if they don't reverse.'

Channel 4 News

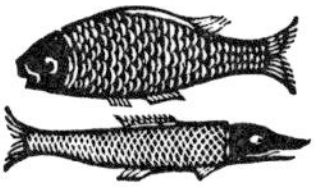

Amis to Larkin:

HOTEL BEAU-SITE, VAR, FRANCE,
9 September 1956

The only annoying thing is the language. Why can't they speak English like everyone else?

'intracticable'

Radio 4

Frank Dixon Graham,
Andrew Graham-Dixon:
parents taking turn and turn about?

Minister accused of sexual misconduct
'had the whip suspended'

Acis
'so wet you can carry
him around in a bucket'
Radio 3 listener

Newsnight:

'Intelligence is not a hundred per cent perfect. It's often scraps or tiny pieces of information... Intelligence officers and police have to make judgments on, very often, impartial information.'

Author on fish:

Helen Scales

'A jigsaw can never be done badly, only slowly'

Kate Romano

‘Box set’
‘poison chalice’
‘close season’
‘mix pickles’
‘ice tea’
‘fry rice’
‘schedule maintenance’
‘detail knowledge’

Samuel Johnson:
‘Burke, sir, is such a man, that if you met him for the first time in a street where you were stopped by a drove of oxen, and you and he stepped aside to take shelter but for five minutes, he’d talk to you in such an extraordinary manner, that, when you parted, you would say, this is an extraordinary man.’

Five universities in Leeds

Password 'too easy to guess':
buggerthisforagame0fsoldiers

'He made an ascent of a subsidiary summit of Baltoro Kangri, claiming a world altitude record with a height of 23,000 ft (7,010 m). However, subsequent measurements have revised his height to 22,322 ft.'

'easy-go-lucky'

William James:

'Common-sense contents itself with the unreconciled contradiction, laughs when it can, and weeps when it must, and makes, in short, a practical compromise, without trying a theoretical solution.'

Robert Musil:

'One must have the courage to live in the midst of moral contradictions.'

William Empson:

'Life consists of maintaining oneself between contradictions that cannot be solved by analysis.'

Lionel Trilling:
'The test of a first-rate intelligence is the ability to hold two opposed ideas in the mind at the same time, and still retain the ability to function.'

'. . . loss of his libraryhood . . .'

'The Law of Non-Contradiction, sometimes also called the Law of Contradiction'
Stanford Encyclopædia of Philosophy

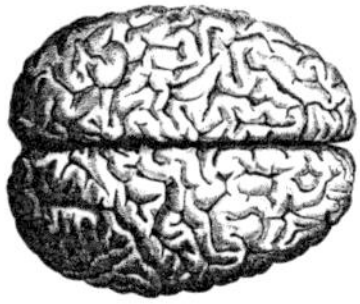

'Public sector borrowing
hit a surplus last month.'
BBC News

'Ill-begotten gains'
Joe Biden

Nine-year-old boy likes girls' shoes and plays girls in school role-play; classmates call him 'transgender', now 'on this journey' to changing sex on the NHS.
(*Obtaining a new credit card:* 'the application journey')

Proposal to make the world
a better place by beheading
everyone who likes selfies as
much as Charles I

'Domestic Abuse
Commissioner'

'The use and abuse of the ball-moulding in the Decorated period in the district between Gloucester and Hereford is remarkable.'
A. E. Housman

'Jelly-mould SUVs'

'Together we can end domestic abuse.'
Website of Network Rail

Book dealer unable to sell to a Scottish library without declaring her Anti-Slavery policy

Harry Potter translated into American for editions there

'an unpresupposing building'

So cold that

'Who blew his nose had clout or fist all
Instead of snivel fill'd with Crystal,
Who drew for Urinal ejection,
Was b'witched into an odd erection.'

Charles Cotton

After the controversy over the statue of Cecil Rhodes above the gates of Oriel College:

Nadhim Zahawi
'Let's elect politicians who stand on a platform saying we'll take statues down.'

Commentator
'. . . giving him a pedestal from which to peddle this apology . . . '

Oxford student
'Black Lives Matter used to be a niche issue, but not now.'

‘Rhymes as pat as butter’
Leigh Hunt

‘He’s an absolutely unique individual, and we need more people like him.’

Radio 4:
‘There is tremendous agreement, at least among myself.’

Placido Domingo accused of
‘inappropriate overtures’